3/21

Arctic Fox

by Grace Hansen

ARCTIC ANIMALS

Abdo Kids Jumbo is an Imprint of Abdo Kids
abdobooks.com

abdobooks.com

Published by Abdo Kids, a division of ABDO, P.O. Box 398166, Minneapolis, Minnesota 55439.
Copyright © 2020 by Abdo Consulting Group, Inc. International copyrights reserved in all countries.
No part of this book may be reproduced in any form without written permission from the publisher.
Abdo Kids Jumbo™ is a trademark and logo of Abdo Kids.

Printed in the United States of America, North Mankato, Minnesota.

102019

012020

 THIS BOOK CONTAINS RECYCLED MATERIALS

Photo Credits: Alamy, iStock, Minden Pictures, Shutterstock

Production Contributors: Teddy Borth, Jennie Forsberg, Grace Hansen
Design Contributors: Dorothy Toth, Pakou Moua

Library of Congress Control Number: 2019941216
Publisher's Cataloging-in-Publication Data

Names: Hansen, Grace, author.

Title: Arctic fox / by Grace Hansen

Description: Minneapolis, Minnesota : Abdo Kids, 2020 | Series: Arctic animals | Includes online
    resources and index.

Identifiers: ISBN 9781532188855 (lib. bdg.) | ISBN 9781532189340 (ebook) | ISBN 9781098200329
    (Read-to-Me ebook)

Subjects: LCSH: Arctic fox--Juvenile literature. | Foxes--Juvenile literature. | Zoology--Arctic regions--
    Juvenile literature. | Snow fox--Juvenile literature. | Arctic--Juvenile literature.

Classification: DDC 599.775--dc23

Table of Contents

The Arctic

The Arctic is the northernmost part of Earth. It is made up of land, the Arctic Ocean, and the **sea ice** that floats on it. The weather there is freezing cold. Any animal that lives in the Arctic is tough!

4

Arctic Foxes

Arctic foxes live throughout the Arctic. They can be found roaming the **tundra**. They often live near the coast.

Arctic foxes have small bodies.

Adults can weigh between 6

and 20 pounds (2.7 and 9.1 kg).

They can be 18 to 42 inches

(46 to 107 cm) long.

Their tails are big and fluffy!

They can wrap their tails around themselves to keep warm.

An Arctic fox has tiny ears and a short snout. This helps keep body heat in.

Fur grows on the bottoms of its feet. This keeps its feet from freezing to the icy ground.

14

In the winter, the foxes' coats are fluffy and white. In the summer months, they shed their fur. Underneath, their coats are thinner and darker in color.

17

Baby Arctic Foxes

Female Arctic foxes have their babies in a den. Usually, 5 to 12 **pups** are born at a time. They are very small at birth.

The **pups** drink their mother's milk and grow. They are ready to leave the den at 2 weeks old. Their parents teach them to hunt.

More Facts

- Arctic foxes can survive in temperatures as low as -58 degrees F (-50 degrees C). That's cold!

- Arctic foxes love to hunt and eat rodents, birds, and fish. They will even eat vegetables!

- When temperatures are really cold and food is scarce, Arctic foxes must be smart. They follow polar bears and eat the bears' leftover food.

Glossary

pup – the young of a fox and some other mammals.

sea ice – frozen ocean water that is typically covered with snow.

snout – the part of an animal's head that sticks out that includes the nose, mouth, and jaws.

tundra – one of the huge plains in the arctic regions of North America, Europe, and Asia. Trees do not grow on the tundra.

Index

Abdo Kids
ONLINE
FREE! ONLINE MULTIMEDIA RESOURCES

Visit **abdokids.com** to access crafts, games, videos, and more!

Use Abdo Kids code

AAK8855

or scan this QR code!